What Our Readers Have Said...

Applicability

"These books are great tools that should be used as guidelines for our everyday supervisory practices. You need to take the time to do a short self-evaluation when reading them."

•

"The Pinpoint Training Series delivers information that could be used in a lot different areas."

•

"The things and problems we deal with everyday are discussed in these books."

Convenience

"I like this because I can take them with me to read at a convenient time. I feel the little time I have to spend in the office is best use on activities that directly relate to revenue opportunities. I like the short amount of time it takes to keep up with these."

•

"I prefer the self-study approach; it fits in with my schedule."

•

"I like the fact that the format allows the books to be reviewed as time permits. All work has been conducted on personal, evening/weekend time."

•

"Easy to use... if you put the time into it."

Challenge

"My thought is that the real value of these books comes into effect when doing the action plans."

•

"I like the fact that the format allows assignments to be reviewed as time permits."

Clarity

"Short and sweet. These books are easy to comprehend."

•

"Easy to use, understand, and reference if needed."

Relevance

"I have enjoyed reading these books. They are relevant to today's work environment and the ongoing change in the way we manage our workforce."

•

"I believe the contents of the Pinpoint series are excellent. It causes one to reflect on the daily dynamics in working with oneself as well as with management and peers."

Leadership Roles & Responsibilities

Pinpoint Leadership Skill Development Training Series

TIMOTHY F. BEDNARZ

MAJORIUM
BUSINESS PRESS

Pinpoint Leadership Skill Development Training Series
"Leadership Roles & Responsibilities"
Timothy F. Bednarz

Graphic design: Monika Pawlak

Majorium Business Press
2025 Main Street
Stevens Point, WI 54481
715.342.1018 • 800.654.4935

ISBN 978-1-882181-39-1

Printed in the United States of America

Introduction

The Pinpoint Leadership Skill Development Training Series is designed for targeted training and education regarding increased improvement in a specific skill or competency.

Each book within this series is designed to be easy to use, understand and apply to your job. It can be used as a basis for training individuals, as a discussion guide or as a personal training tool.

Each chapter within this book discusses a specific concept. When you have completed all eight chapters you should have a 360° perspective of the topic.

Additionally, each chapter is divided into specific sections:

- The first section provides you with an overview of the topic
- The Implications section discusses why the concept is important, and why it is important to learn and apply.
- The Strategies, Tips & Techniques to Apply section teaches how to use and apply the particular concept to your work.
- The Points to Ponder section gives you something to think about or to be discussed with a group setting. These are questions not meant to be immediately answered, but to be pondered over time.
- The Training Activity section provides you with the tools to transfer what you have learned to your job. It is designed to help create an action plan to effectively apply the concept.

Each of the topics in this series is time-tested and proven in the marketplace. They have been used by thousands of employees as training tools. Many of the users have commented that what made these books valuable, was the ability to refer to them when a problem surfaced. They indicated that they remembered reading about the exact problem. They referred back to these books and found an appropriate solution.

You will find them equally valuable as a resource in your professional development library.

Table of Contents

LEARNING OBJECTIVES:

- To identify and apply the elements, factors and principles defining professional leadership roles and responsibilities.
- To overcome problems and pitfalls related to developing and maintaining one's leadership role and responsibilities.
- To apply specific strategies to enhance the development of one's leadership role and position.
- To identify and analyze the various impacts a leader's roles and responsibilities have upon organizational and personal decision making.
- To analyze the expected results and outcomes of developing and maintaining leadership roles and subsequent responsibilities.

1

What Constitutes the Empowered Leader?

There is a pronounced difference between leaders and managers. Managers direct their employees, while leaders motivate and inspire them.

In the business world there are managers who are not leaders and leaders who are not managers. Ideally, managers should also be leaders capable of motivating, empowering, guiding and supporting their team to greater heights of achievement in everything they do.

Specific characteristics and criteria constitute the empowered leader. Their primary goal is to build a highly effective workplace; their actions are consistent to support that end. Positive leadership behavior is the differentiating factor that makes a leader highly effective and indispensable to his or her staff and company.

IMPLICATIONS – WHAT THIS MEANS TO YOU

The specific principles and actions of empowered leadership shift the focus directly to the needs of their employees as a team to the accomplishment of specific management goals. This change in focus allows the leader to realize higher performance from his or her team through empowerment and delegation.

STRATEGIES, TIPS & TECHNIQUES TO APPLY

Empowered leaders are attuned to their employees' expectations of them, while managers tend to focus on meeting specific goals and objectives to increase productivity. A leader's actions are always directed towards four expectations of their employees:

- Security
- Fairness and justice
- A sense of personal involvement
- Fulfillment

Empowered leaders continually work to create strong, efficient, highly effective workforces containing a positive environment of employee trust, respect and acceptance. In order to meet these specific expectations, the following principles and actions can be used.

Moving Away from Control, Toward Empowerment

Empowered leaders always apply the principles of empowerment in order to create a positive workplace environment where the feelings of others are taken into consideration.

Relinquishing total control has often been a weakness for many leaders. This is a natural tendency, as their position requires responsibility and accountability for the results in their department.

Before employees are able to accept a superior's role as leader, managerial control must evolve into empowerment, motivation and delegation. This builds a sense of security, involvement and fulfillment that produces increased results. To formulate a practical empowerment strategy, leaders must:

- Replace control with actions that emphasize all employee input will be taken seriously and given respectful consideration. Managers often like to "play it safe" rather than taking a risk; empowered leaders understand that increased risk from "letting go" comes with increased opportunity.
- Ask for and accept input, assuring it will be acted upon and credit

given when and where due. This technique heightens motivation and performance by bringing trust and loyalty to the fore. Using delegation and cooperation skillfully, builds workplace strength, values and ethics.

- Create a sense of workplace ownership in everything accomplished. Managers often find it easy to stifle creativity in their employees because they don't want to "rock the boat." Empowered leaders understand that change and positive movement ahead must come with some risk attached.

Using Motivation to Replace Ordering

Managers often confuse motivation with the application of a series of negative "can'ts won'ts and don'ts" to maintain workplace effectiveness and structure. Positive motivation focuses on maintaining the four areas of security, fairness and justice, individual involvement and personal fulfillment.

Telling or dictating does not produce the same effects as motivating individuals to want to increase their own performance. To motivate effectively, empowered leaders:

- Learn everything possible about the personalities of their employees.
- Apply specific motivational techniques with each individual employee, not general techniques for all.
- Create a definite relationship between motivation and personal enhancement.
- Apply motivational techniques consistently.
- Demonstrate the motivational factors of cooperation, determination, persistence and the feeling of success in their own daily personal actions. Leaders use their own actions to reinforce and openly display personal motivation for all to observe.

Replace Self-Sufficiency with Cooperation

Many managers find it difficult to delegate due to the pressures of time, the perceived lack of candidates to delegate to and the presumption that they alone know how best to get something accomplished.

The following actions produce a greater cooperative effort and build employee commitment into the workplace atmosphere. These include:

- Know the right individuals to delegate to. Better cooperation comes with identifying and matching the right person's abilities and talents to the specific tasks needing delegation. Take the time to discuss expectations, timelines, objectives and support.
- Demonstrate that cooperative efforts create a sense of ownership in projects and also create shared responsibility for their outcomes.
- Maintain open lines of communication while accepting input seriously in words and actions to produce a cooperative spirit.
- Openly sharing all daily successes. Cheerleading even minor successes creates a unifying atmosphere of caring and cooperation.

POINTS TO PONDER — SOMETHING TO THINK ABOUT

1. How have daily time constraints interfered with your empowered leadership focus? What have been the results of this interference?
2. Have you developed any specific leadership goals as part of your daily activities?

TRAINING ACTIVITY — APPLICATION & ACTION PLAN

Create four columns on a piece of paper and label them accordingly: Security, Fairness and Justice, Personal Involvement, Personal Fulfillment.

1. Under each column, list four specific techniques you can focus upon.
2. Next to the techniques, list one action you can apply to build increased cooperative efforts, trust and loyalty in your employees.

3. Apply these actions consistently.
4. List positive changes you observe that move you closer to becoming an empowered leader.

2

Defining the Roles of the Leader

Managers are often task-oriented, and not necessarily focused on their employees.

Leaders on the other hand are people-oriented; they work through and motivate their employees, utilizing their resources to perform assigned tasks in the most productive and profitable way possible.

Many managers confuse management with leadership, and feel they are automatically leaders because they occupy a position of higher responsibility. While this assumption is often true, many fail to display active leadership qualities. The roles leaders fulfill are different than those of managers, although sound management practices are complementary to effective leadership.

IMPLICATIONS — WHAT THIS MEANS TO YOU

While some individuals are natural leaders, most managers must evolve into leaders both by investing time and effort in developing their abilities and by adapting their management roles to a more flexible, effective leadership style.

Leadership demands a shift in focus from tasks to individuals. Leaders learn how to harness the specific talents of every employee team member in driving efficiency and productivity. While this may appear to be more work than it's worth, effective leaders are able to produce higher levels of productivity with fewer problems than from simply using traditional managing techniques.

STRATEGIES, TIPS & TECHNIQUES TO APPLY

When leaders adhere to specific leadership roles they will foster trust, inward strength and a unity of purpose in the groups under their direction. As leaders, they will embrace their own personal responsibilities, understanding that anything is possible and attainable. They will recognize that each specific element is a stepping stone to the next that ultimately creates a transition from managing to leadership. To define a personal leadership role, the following three principles are critical:

Self-Management

Leaders take complete responsibility for all their actions and decisions. Often leaders must make a decision to challenge rules proven to be detrimental to their overall work environment and the people entrusted to them. The role of a leader is to set ineffective or unproductive rules and procedures aside in favor of those promoting increased cooperation, trust and ownership.

Leaders never waiver in this pursuit. They understand that part of their role is to take risks whenever a policy, procedure or situation hinders progress—and stand by their decisions.

Making improvements often means rocking the boat. While often challenging to the best leaders, this is a substantial part of true leadership. Leaders recognize the status quo often isn't good enough, and that it takes change and creativity to generate improvements.

Leading People

Leaders approach their roles with serious determination. Part of their role is not to dwell on the "rearview mirror," but to look forward. They learn from past mistakes and errors in judgment, but never allow them to affect future opportunities and possibilities. Leaders learn to detach themselves from their circumstances to maintain a clear, forward-thinking perspective.

In order to succeed, leaders must unburden themselves of emotions and perceived limitations that impede attainment of goals and performance. They know past experiences can easily alter good judgment. For a leader, past experiences become the lessons for the future, producing the wisdom to adapt to change.

Leaders know situations or problems will not always fit into neat compartments and have predictable outcomes. They understand and accept that even the most unthinkable changes and devastating occurrences are a possibility, and that their role is to embrace the challenge to overcome them.

Leaders also know they must be flexible in any and all situations, and that looking forward requires creating viable alternatives. They are aware that part of their function is to embrace change and the challenges it brings.

Cultivate the People under Your Direction

The most important role a leader must fulfill is to cultivate, support and nurture employees. Anything can be achieved with fertile enough ground to plant and grow the seeds of accomplishment. To best achieve this end, it is important to:

Learn and remember. Leaders know part of their role is to learn everything about every person under their charge. They make it a point to learn what is important to each, to celebrate special days, achievements and even sadness with outward expressions, incentives, written memos, awards, notes and letters. Nothing builds loyalty and cooperation in employees better than being both professionally and personally attuned to them.

Demonstrate fairness and a cooperative spirit. Leaders work with their employees to maintain high levels of motivation and productive team efforts. They do this by clearly educating their employees on specific procedures, problems and needed skills. Leaders also acknowledge and take seriously the expectations employees have of them. This role builds trust, loyalty and the desire for all to achieve.

Walk the floor—get your hands dirty. Part of a leader's role is to offer help when and where it is needed. This can only be done by personally taking part in tasks and assignments and being an overall active participant in what is going on in their workplace. Knowledge is gathered, problems disclosed and people motivated when leaders fulfill this role. Employees gain respect for leaders who willingly undertake this interaction in a positive fashion rather than view it as an obligation.

POINTS TO PONDER — SOMETHING TO THINK ABOUT

1. How have you previously defined your role as a leader?
2. Do you feel general management practices have interfered with your personal leadership role? If so, how?

TRAINING ACTIVITY — APPLICATION & ACTION PLAN

On a piece of paper write the heading, "My personal leadership role."

1. Write a detailed definition of what constitutes your personal leadership role.
2. Below this, list the specific duties that need to be incorporated into your leadership role. Include those presented.
3. Add other responsibilities you feel are necessary to complete your role as a leader.

3

How Leaders Lead

All leaders have specific characteristics in common. They are decisive, action-oriented and capable of seizing the moment. They see opportunities in the midst of adversity and chaos, and can consider issues from opposing points of view.

Managers generally feel forced to compromise and "go with the flow" to make things easier in the workplace. They often display the general characteristics of self-preservation, anxiousness, aloofness and hesitancy.

The attributes of a leader positively affect their perceptions, attitudes, motivation and drive. These positive effects ensure leaders and their employees will reap tangible benefits including cooperative and creative efforts, decisiveness, loyalty and trust—the main ingredients for success.

IMPLICATIONS – WHAT THIS MEANS TO YOU

The leader's ability to cultivate the aforementioned traits is crucial as they are constantly applied and reinforced in successfully fulfilling their managerial leadership role.

STRATEGIES, TIPS & TECHNIQUES TO APPLY

There are four specific characteristics that will differentiate individuals from being strictly managers and help transform their outlook and attitude toward the role and responsibilities of true leaders.

1. **Appreciation for the power of determination and persistence.**

Managers often start their jobs with determination and persistence, but daily workplace pressures diminish these qualities. Feelings of success are often sporadic and short-lived as new goals are established, new quotas and expectations demanded.

Leaders conversely embrace a dogged, unceasing determination and persistence. This is an intrinsic component of their makeup that shines through all adversity and undertakings. Leader's develop persistence from:

> *Evaluating past experiences of success, no matter how small.* Leaders review all their successes and use these victories to drive them forward. Instead of trying to avoid failure or even expecting negative outcomes, they dwell on their accomplishments in order to create an expectation of further success.
>
> *Their personal values and ethics.* Leaders cling to their values without compromise and use them as a guide in all they do. They blend their ethics into personal values, realizing that their consistent application produces fairness, justice, unfailing confidence and the ability to move beyond problems and negative situations. These values and ethics are continually displayed for all to see.
>
> *Others.* Leaders gain strength from others as well as from themselves. Tackling challenges corporately provides a forum in which to commiserate over failures along the way to achieving desired outcomes. Eventually all will profit from the satisfaction of accomplishment, and leaders use this positive experience to maintain their drive.

2. **Never allowing limitations to hinder success and productivity.**

Managers often encounter seemingly insurmountable roadblocks in carrying out the goals and objectives assigned to them. These obstructions hinder their effectiveness and personal productivity, as time must be spent wading through problems, conflicts and work slowdowns. These frustrations diminish enjoyment of their efforts, work and positions.

Leaders on the other hand know negative attitudes regarding limitations and problems—real or perceived—only work against them. Instead of dwelling on negative attitudes and limitations, they adopt the following philosophy:

- "What no one before us achieved, we will do, no matter what challenges arise, no matter what difficulties stand in the way, no matter what the cost."
- "We will modify, adjust and transform—but will always move ahead. Changes will be seen as opportunities, and we will all work toward the end result of triumphing over the most adverse conditions."
- "Expectations of others will not exceed the expectations of myself." Leaders find they generally expect less from others than from themselves. This drive to meet their own expectations pushes them onward.
- Accomplishment doesn't come from wanting, it comes with the price of trial and error. Wanting something doesn't guarantee it will be secured. Pursuing it comes with attempts that at times will fall short. Subsequent attempts are refined from previous errors in judgment.

3. **Making quick, effective decisions.**

Managers often fall short in quickly identifying solutions to a given problem. A feeling of insecurity often overshadows attempts to develop and embrace change. Managers are often fearful of the consequences their decisions may entail.

Leaders on the other hand fear nothing and move ahead boldly with decisive actions regarding change and direction. They are willing to accept all attendant responsibility. Leaders find that their roadmap to decisiveness includes:

- Viewing all sides of a problem in a short period of time while deciding the best road to take at any particular moment.
- Not allowing fears to overcome their desire to perform.
- Embracing the opportunities all new tasks bring to increase their overall experience and desire to achieve.
- Accepting and embracing challenges on all levels, as, for a leader, challenges equate to success.

4. **Success comes with risk taking.**

Managers often find it easy to stifle creativity in themselves and their employees because they don't want to "rock the boat."

Leaders embrace risk taking with the understanding that risk is the only path to accomplishment. Their attitudes toward taking risks include:

- Understanding that change and positive movement forward always come with some risk attached.
- Knowing that risk comes with elements of opportunity.
- Recognizing the importance of allowing employees to take a risk in order to build their confidence, loyalty, trust and ability to move ahead through mistakes.
- Demonstrating and emphasizing mistakes are a normal process with risk taking, and necessary for growth and success.
- Building a risk taking environment that creates unity of purpose, creativity in solving problems, and a team spirit where solutions, responsibilities and consequences become a shared experience.

POINTS TO PONDER — SOMETHING TO THINK ABOUT

1. Have you ever found yourself compromising your personal beliefs and ethics in order to produce a smoother situation in the workplace? How did you feel? What situation caused this to happen?
2. Are you able to maintain your persistence and determination? What techniques do you use to motivate yourself? Are they always effective? Why or why not?

TRAINING ACTIVITY — APPLICATION & ACTION PLAN

Write down a situation you are experiencing in the workplace that continually disrupts your ability to lead effectively.

1. Look at the problem from a minimum of three varying viewpoints you have not previously considered.
2. Write solutions to the problem from each of the three perspectives.
3. Select one solution that appears to be the most effective and apply it to the problem.
4. Observe how this decision impacts and improves your personal performance or workplace outcomes.

4

Dealing with Superiors Who Are Not Leaders

One of the most frustrating dilemmas facing a leader is dealing with a superior who is either not a leader or does not share the corporate vision to change. This is a volatile situation fraught with danger to the personal success of the leader and his or her career.

All organizational change has its own pitfalls. When a company changes its management style from a managerial bureaucracy to an open style of leadership, there will be certain individuals in power who will completely resist the change. They may be guarding their own territory and reluctant to surrender their personal power base, or simply too inflexible to change after many years in the organization.

IMPLICATIONS — WHAT THIS MEANS TO YOU

Superiors reticent to change have the ability to stop a leader's progress even though this is counter to the organization's overall goals. If leaders must deal with this reality, they must learn to work within the constraints placed upon them and use the system to their advantage.

STRATEGIES, TIPS & TECHNIQUES TO APPLY

The Problem

Organizational change has been mandated from the senior levels of management, but a leader has a superior who is blocking its successful implementation. They are resistant to any change and actively interfere with the leader's ability to manage his or her team.

In these situations, the superior does not share the corporate vision or is guarding their own territory from an intrusion into their power base. Additionally, they may not see any way to personally benefit from the change.

The Consequences

The consequences of a superior's active interference in a leader's performance of their responsibilities can be serious. These individuals might withhold information, undermine the leader's position and cover up their mistakes in an effort to consolidate their personal base of power.

This results in demotivating the workforce who may hear the corporate mandates, but are exposed to the superior's contrary words and actions. Due to the mixed message, they don't see the possibility for change nor do they feel that management is "walking the walk."

Despite the personal consequences, leaders cannot allow their superior's actions to destroy the morale and productivity they wish to create.

The Solution

Leaders must work within the organizational system to resolve this problem. They cannot sit still and watch their work collapse due to the personal agenda of a single individual. There are several simultaneous courses of action a leader can take to resolve this situation.

Discussions with the superior

The leader can sit down with his or her superior to discuss the organizational mandate and how their actions are interfering with the leader's workplace morale and performance. The point is to arrive at a consensus of action both parties can agree to that allows the leader to move forward. This may include the superior loosening his or her boundaries and limits, or to agree to a limited, controlled amount of risk.

Leaders should avoid any emotional confrontation and solely deal with the facts when discussing the issues with a reluctant superior.

Search for a champion

Leaders can search for a champion within the organization to assist them to overcome the superior's resistance. A champion would typically be senior to both, who could act as a mentor and confidant to the leader. In an informal role, this individual may be able to bring appropriate pressure to bear on the superior to change.

Work with other leaders

Several leaders under the management of a reluctant superior can work together to bring pressure to bear on the superior to change. If this fails and there is a need to go over the superior's head, there will be more credibility if all employee leaders are working together to solve the problem. If they approach senior management as a team with a documented problem they are experiencing with the superior, it is more likely they will advance their cause and be able to relax the constraints they are forced to work within.

POINTS TO PONDER — SOMETHING TO THINK ABOUT

1. What has been your experience with superiors that have created roadblocks to your leadership success?
2. How have you previously dealt with a reluctant superior?

TRAINING ACTIVITY — APPLICATION & ACTION PLAN

Develop a plan to identify and foster a champion within your organization.

1. Identify several potential candidates.
2. Identify reasons why they should champion your cause.
3. What is their motivation?
4. What do you have in common with each possible champion?
5. How will you approach each one?
6. How will you nurture them?

5

Developing Specific Leadership Roles and Responsibilities

A leader's specific roles are determined through the four basic leadership responsibilities of directing, coaching, supporting and delegating. Specific responsibilities will fall into one of these four categories. In leadership practice, one must master skills in all areas in order to effectively lead others under their direction.

Effective leadership is not happenstance; it follows specific rules revolving around these four basic areas of responsibility.

IMPLICATIONS — WHAT THIS MEANS TO YOU

Leadership skills can be learned and developed, even if an individual does not have a natural tendency toward leadership. More importantly, once learned and applied, these rules make a leader more effective and productive as he or she learns to work, direct and guide others toward the mutual accomplishment of goals and objectives.

STRATEGIES, TIPS & TECHNIQUES TO APPLY

Developing strengths in each of the four leadership roles allows a leader to read specific situations accurately and know what communication style is best applied.

Directing

Directing refers to how to keep work tasks and activities on the right track. A leader's direction is what makes or breaks problem solving as well as determines the effectiveness of an approach to an assignment or task, the maintaining of momentum until its completion, and whether it is done by deadline. There are several ways to generate good direction techniques. These include:

> *Explain things completely and include the 'why's.'* Leaders learn early on that the best way to gain support and trust from their employees is to explain all things in their entirety. Once people understand why something is important or necessary, they generally rally to the call of that which needs to be done or addressed.
>
> *Remain visible.* Leaders understand the power of their presence at all times. Nothing deflates the workforce's motivation and desire to achieve more than to be left on their own with no visible means of support or direction.
>
> *Objectively consider opposing points of view.* Leaders consider situations, problems and solutions from various viewpoints, as the input from as many individuals as possible expands their capabilities to effectively frame their direction.

Coaching

Coaching refers to when a leader knows where he or she wants to go and remains in control of the task but needs to lead others in developing a mutual support network. Coaching instills the desire to achieve and builds a dialogue bridge between the leader and those under his or her charge. This motivates employees and positively changes attitudes toward the work assignment. To do this effectively a leader must make an effort to:

> *Incorporate the word 'we' into all conversations.* Effective leaders eliminate the word "I" because it denotes a singular rather than cooperative effort. The very meaning of the term "coaching" implies a team effort.
>
> *Listen for objections and areas of misunderstanding.* Effective leaders who coach well develop the skill of eliminating objections by developing an effective dialogue and creating clear and concise responses.

Offer explanations addressing the 'why's, what's and how's' of the problem or task at hand. Good coaching depends upon complete understanding. Motivation and confidence comes from understanding the expectations a leader has of those involved in a given task, assignment or problem solving situation.

Supporting

Managers cannot be effective leaders unless they actively hone their supporting skills. People look warmly on leaders who actively work to support them emotionally as well as physically. When leaders actively work to support the people under their charge they:

Acknowledge individual efforts with comments of praise and positive support. Leaders are not afraid to say "thank you," or "you're doing a great job," or whatever it takes to instill confidence in an individual.

Disclose their own feelings openly and honestly. Leaders are not afraid to reveal their "inner self." Trust and loyalty are built on disclosing inward feelings, concerns and desires. Readily and honestly opening up builds encouragement and perseverance on both sides.

Never hesitate to ask, 'What's wrong?' Leaders allow themselves to get into the thick of a situation or task, and are quick to share the decision making responsibility, but know when to relinquish control in order to gain extra participation and involvement.

Delegating

Leaders know and understand their people. They know their strengths and weaknesses as well as what motivates and frustrates them. Effective delegating relies on the ability to select the proper person for the specific task or role. Leaders develop good delegation skills by:

Briefing the delegate. Leaders leave nothing to chance when they delegate. When delegating, it is vital to explain exactly what expectations the leader has of the delegated individual.

Having confidence in the person they select. Leaders do not select individuals for an assignment according to their job descriptions or the salaries they command, they look for people with the skills, abilities, perseverance and motivation to get the job done and done well.

Not abdicating responsibility, but allowing individuals to decide a best course of action for themselves. Leaders monitor and weigh these individual decisions, but never advance their own leadership position for a particular course of action unless they assess it to be the best one.

POINTS TO PONDER — SOMETHING TO THINK ABOUT

1. Do you experience a personal weakness in any of the four leadership responsibilities discussed? What steps can you take to improve in one of these areas?
2. How do you currently motivate your workforce to gain their active participation?

TRAINING ACTIVITY — APPLICATION & ACTION PLAN

On a piece of paper create a table, six columns by four or more rows. Head each with Direction, Coaching, Delegation, and Support.

1. Under each heading write down what you currently are doing to fulfill each responsibility.
2. Place a checkmark by the ones that work most effectively for you.
3. Think creatively to expand certain actions and list them under each column.
4. Practice applying your creative ideas to increase your leadership proficiency in each of these four responsibility categories.
5. Write down the positive effects you observe that enhance your personal effectiveness.

6

Leading by Example

There are specific ways leaders exhibit an untarnished example. The key is to project an aura that is genuine, consistent and unwavering. Belief in a leader comes from the trust and respect they command. The example they set to gain this approval and loyalty originates in openly and continually displaying their personal integrity, curiosity and passion.

IMPLICATIONS — WHAT THIS MEANS TO YOU

A leader's efforts will ultimately succeed or fail based on the examples they set for others. Their open, easily seen examples have the greatest effect on gaining support, trust and motivation. They consistently display a zeal for their work, beliefs and ideas, and weigh all actions with fairness, justice and integrity. Using their personal values and honesty, curiosity and passion as their guidelines, they are able to motivate people effectively.

STRATEGIES, TIPS & TECHNIQUES TO APPLY

Maintaining consistent examples in each of the three areas of integrity, curiosity and passion is key.

Integrity

Leaders recognize the three elements constituting personal integrity, and continually work to master each of them. These are:

> *Self-knowledge.* Understanding oneself is no easy task. Leaders never lie to themselves because it destroys their chance to lead successfully. Setting an example takes confidence and courage: as much as drawing upon their strengths to the fullest, it requires leaders to admit to specific areas of weakness. Leaders understand the importance of bringing others "into their world" to fill the gaps their personal weaknesses create. This does not require the sharing of every possible piece of personal information, only demonstrating the understanding that people—leaders included—have strengths and weaknesses.
>
> *Ability to examine personal thoughts and actions.* Integrity is based upon honestly examining one's own personal thoughts and actions. Leaders exhibit a steadfast devotion to their principles and values, and never compromise them to please others. They send a clear message that the way to become self-defeated is to ignore conscience in order to fit another's expectations and desires or to gain acceptance.
>
> *Maturity.* Leaders understand that setting an untarnished example is not accomplished simply through issuing orders. They know their power comes from past experiences of failure and success, following examples of great leaders and growing from lessons learned. Because of the wisdom gained, they allow others to make errors in judgment and grow from them. Displaying maturity allows others to become confident, observant, dedicated and capable of working with and learning from others.

Curiosity

Leaders explore every unopened door because of the potential opportunity behind them. Their desire to learn must continuously set an example for others if they wish to motivate and change them in a positive way. Setting a model example for curiosity requires:

Daring to learn. Leaders want to openly suggest ways to build a desire for learning. Learning gives everyone the confidence to forge ahead into new avenues of thought, actions and possibilities. This takes them out of the traditional box to observe things from various perspectives. This is a necessary attribute to try out new ideas and replace former, less productive ways of doing things. These efforts bring about greater rewards. Daring means to accept challenges without holding back or thinking about negative consequences.

Risk taking. Leaders demonstrate the importance of taking risks. Risk taking allows individuals to experiment and try new approaches without limitations attached. Leaders emphasize that risk taking builds character and the desire to persist. It allows everyone under their charge to overcome obstacles others may find extremely difficult. Mistakes are embraced and used as reference points for growth. Limiting risk taking limits personal achievement!

Embracing failure and the errors that cause it. To set an untarnished example, leaders need to acknowledge and stress the importance of failure—often a necessary component in obtaining positive results. Past experiences of failure and the reasons behind them become the cornerstone of success. It is a leader's responsibility to openly embrace failure and not display fear of its consequences. Others will follow, as persisting in the face of failure sets the course and direction for commitment, confidence and trust.

Passion

Leaders understand passion by knowing themselves. In order to lead by example, they must know who they are, what they want to do, exactly where they want to go and why. Passion is structured around three elements:

A direction and purpose. Passion is based upon the understanding of one's selected course of direction and purpose, knowing where it is he or she wants to go. Leaders set an untarnished example by voicing their goals and direction as often as practical in order to both influence others and keep themselves on target.

Attaining desires, hopes and dreams. Leaders demonstrate their passion through desires, hopes and aspirations. They know there is no future without hopes and dreams. Leaders take their personal passion and transmit it by giving hope and inspiration to all people under their charge.

Embracing a love for their profession. Leaders demonstrate their passion by openly displaying a love for their work and the promises held by the future. They combine positive expectations for life's possibilities with a love of their profession. Leaders send a clear, daily message of what the world of work can offer to those who pursue it. They emphasize that work and goals are the way to achieve one's dreams.

POINTS TO PONDER — SOMETHING TO THINK ABOUT

1. What have you specifically done daily in the areas of integrity, curiosity or passion to set an untarnished example? Have you observed any positive changes?
2. In what area(s) do you feel you need to improve your example? Why?

TRAINING ACTIVITY — APPLICATION & ACTION PLAN

Select one of the three areas discussed in which you would like to strengthen your example.

1. List suggestions, ideas and personal actions you can use to set a better example.
2. Check off daily where you have set the personal example, why you did it and how it was received.
3. Evaluate the results at the end of the week. Are your examples having an impact?

7

Monitoring Your Leadership Role

Sound leadership includes continually and objectively taking inventory of oneself. This is not as easy as it appears, because leaders inherently have high levels of self-confidence and often believe they are strong in most areas relating to their leadership role. Even though this quality is important for leaders to fulfill their role effectively, it often obscures specific areas needing improvement.

IMPLICATIONS — WHAT THIS MEANS TO YOU

When leaders honestly assess their performance, they will set goals for improvement. By responding to precise questions in six specific categories it becomes easier to determine areas for improvement that might otherwise be overlooked. These areas and questions need to be addressed carefully in order to improve one's performance in their leadership role.

STRATEGIES, TIPS & TECHNIQUES TO APPLY

It is important for leaders to honestly evaluate themselves in the areas of:

- Establishing a core belief system
- Prioritizing tasks

- Developing methods for monitoring workplace progress
- Giving clear and detailed instructions
- Promoting responsibility
- Improving the overall workplace environment

In order to pinpoint specific areas of strengths and weaknesses, print out the following evaluation areas and questions and write "yes" or "no" before each number.

Establishing a core belief system

1. Do you continually prepare your employees for impending changes by effectively discussing and defending why they are necessary?
2. Do you review procedures and results with your employees on a regular basis?
3. Do your employees know where your direction is taking them?
4. Do your employees understand why it is important to achieve set goals?
5. Do your employees understand and accept established standards for performance and are they complying with workplace rules?

Prioritizing tasks

1. Are your priorities flexible?
2. Do you model the importance of organizational skills to your employees?
3. Do you set daily priorities?
4. Are your employees a daily top priority in terms of their needs and concerns?
5. Do you take an active role in helping employees prioritize their tasks and assignments?

Monitoring workplace progress

1. Do you keep daily records and check off items that move workplace progress forward?
2. Do you have at least one weekly meeting to discuss performance progress and/or timeline implications?
3. Do you consult with individuals that need to increase overall performance on a regular basis?
4. Are you able to determine reasons behind a lack of performance in most of your employees who aren't meeting expectations?
5. Do you motivate using various leadership styles that meet specific individual needs?

Giving detailed instructions clearly

1. Are you allowing adequate time for discussions, asking questions and addressing particular concerns and specific issues that arise?
2. Do you address all the "why's, how's and when's" of assignments and tasks?
3. Do all employees understand why particular procedures are necessary?
4. When plans, goals and objectives are detailed, are they completely understood by all involved?
5. Do you listen to employees carefully and anticipate potential problems or complications in assignments or tasks and take appropriate action before they actually arise?

Promoting responsibility

1. Do you give adequate feedback to employees to build development of responsibility?
2. Do you use motivational techniques to help build the desire to accept responsibility in your employees?
3. Do you assign tasks and responsibilities equally among all employees?

4. Do you encourage your employees to take risks without fear of negative consequences?
5. Do you delegate responsibilities whenever possible to the most qualified individual?

Improving the overall workplace environment

1. Do you celebrate individual successes, great and small?
2. Do you put forth daily efforts to make assignments and tasks more enjoyable for everyone involved?
3. Do you encourage cooperative efforts and input in planning the goals for the direction you wish to take?
4. Do you work to stimulate creativity and "out of the box" thinking?
5. Do you make sure to give each employee one-on-one time throughout each week?

POINTS TO PONDER — SOMETHING TO THINK ABOUT

1. Are there any additional questions you can think of that can be used to evaluate your leadership role?
2. Did you find more areas needing improvement than you first thought before taking this leadership performance evaluation?

TRAINING ACTIVITY — APPLICATION & ACTION PLAN

If you answered "No" to any question(s) in each of the categories listed, make it a point to identify and apply ways to improve in these areas.

1. List the questions you answered "No" to.
2. Underneath each question write down several ideas you can use to

improve your personal role performance.

3. On another sheet of paper, make a separate list of your ideas. Check off each one you apply to improve your role performance.
4. Review this idea evaluation weekly to note any positive changes by putting a "plus" sign next to each one you improve upon.

8

The Leader as a Cheerleader

A challenge leaders face is how to effectively motivate their people and keep personal performance standards high, work assignments stimulating, and directional efforts on course. Leaders need to have several techniques at their fingertips to maintain momentum while moving positively forward.

IMPLICATIONS – WHAT THIS MEANS TO YOU

Leaders make concentrated efforts to motivate employees by encouraging them to develop and grow in their work. Emotional resistance is eliminated when the right motivational techniques are used consistently.

Three vital motivational tools that work effectively in most situations are reassuring, challenging and empathizing. When leaders apply these motivational tools they have better success in improving employee performance, stimulating workplace creativity and reducing individual anxiety.

STRATEGIES, TIPS & TECHNIQUES TO APPLY

In order to offer greater tangible benefits to employees and have them produce effective outcomes leaders can motivate by reassuring, challenging and empathizing. These motivational techniques make individuals feel better about their personal worth, challenge them to participate fully, and align tasks and goals with individual needs and desires. Building techniques around these include:

Motivational Reassuring

This motivational technique is effective for helping employees cope with workplace stress and challenges. The key is to motivate by using specific positive actions and verbal support.

> Leaders focus on motivating by "cheerleading" employees onward in a supportive role. The main goal is to build commitment through influencing them to participate fully. This reduces worry and stress that they will not be able to perform properly or to the leader's expectations. This is accomplished in part through suggesting ways to make tasks and assignments easier and offering shortcuts to eliminate frustrations.
>
> Leaders find a good motivational technique is to let employees know that a certain amount of stress is beneficial because it helps optimize productivity. With that in mind, they disclose all details of what is going to happen to each person involved in a task, project or outcome as much as is predictable. Encouraging employees in their efforts as they move one small step at a time is essential. Positive statements about small successful accomplishments work well to overcome personal insecurity.
>
> Another good motivational technique is to help employees recharge physically and emotionally. This can be accomplished by easing up on their workload occasionally, or by offering "perks" when and where a leader feels it is appropriate. The idea is to move the individual's energy level away from work so renewed bursts of energy can take place.

Motivational Challenging

Motivational challenging works effectively to reduce complacency. Challenging allows employees to be less focused on their own personal wants and problems and more focused on the priorities of the workplace. Motivational techniques need to be focused on the following:

Overcoming an employee's insecurity level in a positive manner is a challenge for many leaders. This can best be accomplished by creating both positive and negative outcomes directly related to individual performance. Leaders find linking performance targets to bonuses or to other intrinsic rewards works well.

Effective leaders know that challenging employees sometimes requires motivating by applying "tough love." They motivate by not allowing themselves to shelter the people under their direction from reality. One technique to keep employees motivated is to engineer a crisis by allowing employee apathy to lead to a fall, rather than protecting them from negative consequences. Experience can become one of the most powerful motivators.

One powerful motivator to challenge employees and get them more involved is through the sharing of information on situations, new procedures and changes that are occurring in the workplace. Leaders understand not sharing important information regarding decisions and changes hinders employees and forces them to function in a negative, reactive state. A leader's goal is to maintain a proactive workplace climate.

Motivational Empathy

This technique is based upon listening to an employee's side of an issue, sharing viewpoints, and providing positive interaction. Leaders must first understand how employees feel. Motivational empathy techniques are effective to build commitment. Leaders align goals and objectives with specific needs and concerns.

Leaders must win the confidence and trust of the people under them. In order to motivate, leaders need to fully understand their employees. This involves gaining an understanding of their perspectives on problems, fears, beliefs and workplace situations. Leaders can then develop strategies to motivate in a positive way to overcome resistance, which then develops a feeling of trust and security within their followers.

Listening is a very effective way to motivate. Not disputing views or perceptions builds higher levels of encouragement. There are times when leading people means walking or working alongside them while saying nothing. Listening allows time to observe and develop strategies to help increase confidence and productivity. To motivate effectively, it is important not to overwhelm employees with a leader's personal power, control and confidence. Listening does this.

Sharing quality time with employees is essential to motivate effectively. This includes personal interaction time in order to discuss and share feelings that are important to the employee. Leaders also find it motivational to share their personal feelings. Taking quality time to exhibit kindness, openness, compassion and genuine concern holds more power to motivate than many other techniques combined.

POINTS TO PONDER — SOMETHING TO THINK ABOUT

1. What style of motivation mentioned above do you apply most often?
2. How often do you use these three types of motivation? Are there any particular factors that prevent you from applying them consistently?

TRAINING ACTIVITY — APPLICATION & ACTION PLAN

Observe one individual employee over the course of a week or two.

1. Write down the individual's name.
2. Next to his or her name write down what type of motivation you believe will be most effective to use with that individual.

3. Observe whether the employee responds favorably to your motivational technique.
4. If not, continue to work toward positive results by using a new technique.

About the Author

Timothy F. Bednarz, Ph.D. is CEO of the American Management Development Group, Inc. For over 20 years he has researched, designed and authored hundreds of learning and development programs used by Fortune 1000 companies.

He is also the author of *Great! What Makes Leaders Great. What They Did, How They Did It and What You Can Learn from It* (2011).

Speaking Availability

Timothy F. Bednarz, Ph.D. is available for speaking engagements for your next meeting or association event. He can be contacted at 800-654-4935 or by e-mail at timothy.bednarz@majorium.com.

Bulk Sales

Bulk sales of this book or any other titles available from Majorium Business Press. Inquiries can be directed to sales@majorium.com, or by phone at 800-6654-4935.

Quick Order Form

Fax orders: 715-342-1118. Send this form.

Telephone orders: Call 800-654-4935 toll-free. Have your credit card ready.

Email orders: sales@majorium.com

Postal orders: Majorium Business Press, 2025 Main Street, Stevens Point, WI 54481, USA.

Please send the following books:

____

____

____

____

Please send more FREE information on:

❑Catalog ❑Speaking/Seminars ❑Mailing Lists ❑Consulting

Name: ____

Address: ______________________________________

City: ____________________ State: _____ Zip: ________

Telephone: ____________________________________

Email address: _________________________________

Sales tax: Please add 5.5% for products shipped to Wisconsin addresses.

Shipping by air:

United States: $4.00 for first book and $2.00 for each additional product.

International: $9.00 for first book; $5.00 for each additional product (estimate).

Made in United States
Cleveland, OH
06 November 2026

47678353R10030